Text Copyright © 2015 by Montrell D Goss
Illustrations Copyright © 2015 by Shawniece Carr
All rights reserved. No part of this book may be used or reproduced in any manner whatsoever without written permission except in the case of brief quotations embodied in critical articles and reviews. Printed in the United States of America.

Mixed Feelings

By Montrell "God's Instrument" Goss

Cover Page By: Shawniece Carr

Success: Acknowledging self-worth in your everyday life by reaching your full potential to accomplish all goals. Not being defeated, but rather defeating the world against all odds. Success cannot be bought, but can be worth a lot. I am a witness that dreams do come true; so live your dream and be successful. Don't let yesterday stop you from being a better person today.

God's Instrument

Bio

"My heart overflows with a beautiful thought! I will recite a lovely poem to the king, for my tongue is like the pen of a skillful poet." (PSLAM 45:1 NLT)

Montrell grew up in a single parent household with three older brothers and a younger sister. Him being the youngest, growing up without a dad really affected him. Living in the cold streets of Portland, a city with not much to do, Montrell tried to occupy his time by playing sports and spending time with his family. As an adolescent, Montrell spent most of his time in bible club and church. As the years went by Montrell started to get stronger in faith. By the age of nineteen Montrell got serious about his writing.

You see everybody has a story to tell but some people just don't know how to tell it. Montrell was one of those people. Until one day God spoke to him and said, "It's easier to get your feelings out if you write them down on paper." After that he began to write a book. By the age of twenty he released his first book called "Judgment Day." In 2011 he released his second book "I'm Not a Writer I Am Poetry" and in 2013 his book "From My Pain to My Passion" was released. Montrell's goal is to win souls, make disciples, and help people release feelings that they hold within. He believes that people shouldn't let yesterday stop them from being better people today. All and all, Montrell wants to show that through everything you go through in life there will always be a better day.

Table of Contents

Dedication	12
Determination Or Motivation?	13
Questions	15
Mind Games	17
Price Or Passion?	19
Take The Bait	21
Last Chance	23
Make A Change	25
My Dreams Is My Reality	27
Good Enough	29
Take It For What It Is	31
Mater Piece	32

Help Wanted	33
Addicted	35
God, We Blame you!	37
I Blame Us!	38
Use To Tell Me	41
Hurting Inside	43
Man… I Need A Drink!	45
I Wish	47
I'm Tired	48
Mind Racing	50
Thoughts	52
If I Was Rich	54
No Words	56

Who's Burning You?	57
Friends Or Nightmares?	59
Let It Out	61
Share It	63
Good Will	65
No Money	67
Off To The Races	69
Mixed Feelings	71
You Gotta Go	73
As Far As It Goes	75
Don't Quit	77
He's There	79
Thousand Words Intro	80

Thousand Words	81
Bonus Poems	87
Bully by God's Instrument	88
Acceptance by God's Instrument	90
Controversy by God's Instrument	92
Heart To Heart by God's Instrument	94
Stop Lying by God's Instrument	96
Broken by God's Instrument	98
My Proverbs 31 by God's Instrument	100
Why Me Intro by God's Instrument	102
Why Me? (Joy) by God's Instrument	103
Why Me? (Fear) by God's Instrument	106
Restored by God's Grace	108

Character, Courage, and Commitment

    by Rebecca Taylor   110

Silent Cry by Duoshun Pledgure   112

Young Boy by God's Instrument   114

Erase These Thought by God's Instrument   116

To The Top by God's Instrument   118

Alter Call by God's Instrument   119

The Prayer by God's Instrument   121

Share Your Story   123

Share Your Story   124

Share Your Story   125

Share Your Story   126

Share Your Story   127

Dedication

Usually I dedicate my books to someone that has affected my life in a certain way, but this time I'm dedicate this one to myself because I have been dealing with mixed feelings, addicted to money, sex, and living life like everyone else. I know every poem in this book isn't about me but a few of them are. As I wrote it I felt bad reading it, got convicted, and never understood how reading a poem could expose who you really are. Writing really helps me, especially because it helps to release the truth about me. Shows me different life styles changes that should be made, brought me closer to God, gave me more faith and understanding to just focus on how God views me. I hope reading this book helps you, just like it is helping me and put your trust in God. You will never know what he has planned for your life if you talk to him. Be patient, wait, and see... I LOVE MYSELF!

Determination Or Motivation?

Is my determination my motivation to be who I need to be, or am I motivated because I'm determined to see what I need to see.

Just because you make it to the top of the mountain and you can see way down below doesn't mean you understand the other side, because sometimes what you see is not really clear until you begin to get closer then the realness starts to appear.

Like for me, I wrote a book, got it published, thought I was the man like I made it, this is it for me. Until I read Matthew 28:19-20 19 (Therefore go and make disciples of all nations baptizing them in the name of the Father and of the Son and of the Holy Spirit).

That touched my heart and it changed what writing a book really meant to me. It gave me a clear vision of my gift, showed me different ways to following my calling. Had to work harder, no games, no procrastination, and had to quit all the stalling. My eyes are open, my vision was a little blurry but I have to continue on my mission, my feet hurt, I'm tired but I will not stop even if kills me. If I started, trust and believe I will finish. My hearts in this, I will finish I have to find my motivation, there's a lot of obstacles, a lot of ups and downs but they won't stop me. I'm ready to take down anything and everything that's put in front of me, anything that I'm facing. My mind is everywhere, heart racing, feet moving because I'm still determined. The other side is near, the finish line is clear. Hard work will pay off, God spoke and said, "Keep going don't give up my son your time is coming."

Questions

What's life without purpose? What's praise without worship? What's joy without pain? And what's the point of dancing in the sunshine? If you're scared to go singing in the rain. How you gonna recover? If you scared to uncover. Your pain, your hurt, and all the things you need to search and discover. How do you progress? If you scared of change? And how you say you a child of God? But the things of the world you do the same. How you gonna ask for forgiveness? Then turn around and do the same. And how you gonna keep living life? If you scared to admit your problems, repent, and face your shame. How you gonna be a leader? If you always been scared to follow. And how you gonna face today? If you're worried about the fears of tomorrow.
So many "how's" in life, so why don't you think hard and figure out what "how's" you are facing. Pray ask God for

help and be patient, soon those "how's" will start to

disappear and those questions of how? Will start erasing.

Mind Games

My mind is playing tricks on me, lost focus, got double vision. Go this way, do that, seems like every move I make is the most important decision, of my life. Crying because I'm confused about theses voices in my head, don't know which one is wrong and which one is right. Do this it's good for you, go that way that's the best path for you, and is all I'm hearing. Questioning myself like is this God or the enemy? Because that's the only thing I'm fearing. You see sometimes we do bad things that feels good so much, that eventually we start to convince ourselves that what we're doing is right. Losing sight of our mission on earth and what God has planned for our lives. Quickly you gain focus you PUSH! And ask God for his guidelines to get you on that right path again. Pray Until Something Happens and when something's does you keep praying so you will be prepared just in case you're faced with this mind set again.

Price Or Passion?

Are you doing this for price or the passion? Trying to build up the kingdom or maybe your just trying to buy a mansion? And I'm just speaking the truth within asking questions that people are afraid of, so they reframe from asking. Really, I'm just trying to get to know you, see where your hearts at. Seeing if you gonna get that depart from me I never knew you, or well done good and faithful servant when Jesus returns, or what I like to call the great come back. Just because you think you're living right and you do a few good deeds day and night, doesn't guarantee you a spot in Heaven if you was to leave this Earth tonight. Doing God's work is great and all, but we still have to have a relationship with Jesus, we think because we do all these great things in the world that's all God needs to be pleased with us. Think again, God still wants to see your church life, how your living and are you trying to mimic Christ life, within knowing you will never be perfect but you trying your hardest to keep your act right. 20/20 vision on God to keep your sight right, praying and reading your bible daily to keep you knowledge of how life should be right. So find the real reason why you do what you do, listen to your heart, price or passion? It's totally up to you.

Take The Bait

My passion is everlasting and my passion is in me, so does that mean I will live forever, everlasting, or will I die one day? Hmmm I guess we shall see. If I die what will they remember? Or better question will they even remember me? I'm trying to make history before I'm history so every day I strive to be the best I can be. My life was already planned out, in this world I'm just living, playing the cards I was dealt with no cheating because God is the one that was doing the dealing. I'm not no fish but I'm biting, the pad and pen was the bait, I snagged the line, tried to pull away but God reeled me in fast, so that I wouldn't escape. Shake or break the line that kept me close, I'm just glad when I was finally caught it was by the one that knows me the most. A lot of time God catches us, reels us in, and right when we get to the shore we bite the line, going back to our old lives because we believe we have so much more time, on this earth. Not realizing we living in our last days, hoping not to be left behind but we continue to live in our old ways. So try it out if you bite the bait don't resist let God catch you, you never know what he has planned or what he has in store just for you.

Last Chance

I woke up and asked God what needs to be different, my life feels like it's on a stand still there has to be something that I'm forgetting. I've messed up in the past, God gave me a second chance and what did I do with it? Went back to my selfish ways, my selfish desires, everything that I did in the past that ruined it. So why should God give me another one, so I can keep messing up. It's like I'm blind to change like I can't just move on and let what's done be done. It's like I'm playing with God, I'm asking for forgiveness, asking God to help me, and change my spirit. He does but I run away, far away, it's like I'm scared I don't even want to be near it. I can hear Gods voice speaking to me all time I'm just too hard headed to listen, even though I hear it. Guess I feel like I got all the time in world, not realizing God will soon return and tell me how I was on this earth and show me my life and how I lived it. I don't want to be left behind hopefully when I walk up the stairway to heaven God will let me pass through the pearly gates, but some changes need to be made, not now but right now, I need to get my life straight. No more narrow roads I have to stay focus on the path God has paved for me. As shameful as it is to ask God for another chance, I pray he stays near and for my sins He's forgiving me.

Make A Change

God showed me my dream, I woke up he showed me my vision. Created a different life style for me he even changed the way I was living. Couldn't do certain things no more had to let things go, get rid of it. Ever had to stop certain friendships, cut all ties, approach them face to face, had to tell them our friendship I'm putting an end to it. Labeled them as a distraction and I now see my vision, I have to move forward. Sorry if they feel like I'm turning my back on them but life is life, and living this same life I'm kind of starting to get bored. Drinking every weekend, partying every night, arguing in the clubs sometimes even leads to fist fights. Instead I should be in church every weekend, praying every night, out in the world spreading the gospel, on my Matthew 5:13-16 mission, becoming the salt and the light. Making a change is hard, but trust in God you will be alright. Open up your heart to God's love when

I got it, it was love at first sight. I love my new life what more can I ask for, God has blessed me with many different gifts and talents this is my forth book I'm staying humble and being patient because I know this isn't it. God is pushing me to stay focus and see what else He has in store, and I'm glad He closed many and the ones I'm supposed to walk through he's opening up those doors.

My Dream is My Reality

I'm out here living my dream while some of y'all still resting, and even if I don't ever make a dollar off these books I still take this gift I have as a blessing. It has got me through some tough times, even has got me out of certain situations. Was sad at some point got real angry one time but I went to my outlet my writing with no second guessing. I always say a little prayer before I pick up my pen and pad. Because I need a clear mind, a little motivation and some guidance from my father, Jesus Christ, my dad. Never thought I would be at this point in my life where every day when I wake up instead of going somewhere and clocking in. I get to sit at my kitchen table grab me some breakfast and think of my next poem to write, go out in the world and do a few shows, visit places, and do some motivational speaking, God blessed me for my poetry to be my job so there is no days off some days I don't even have time for sleeping. This is book number four and after this I pray my dream continues, and after I retire from poetry, I will have started a great legacy, one they will honor and I hope this will be a career my children would want to get into.

Good Enough

Sometimes I wake up and I don't even have the urge write, frightened by the world views, thoughts of us living in our last days got me deep thought like, will I make it into heaven gates or will I get left behind blinding by the fire of hells lights. Cooking in hell's kitchen, playing in the Devils playground, got me mind bothered, spinning, doing a three sixty, ending where I started at. So I guess it's true, what's goes around comes back around. Knowing half of that three sixty is where I should be at in life, one eighty, a complete change, but it's crazy how you change for the better and your family and friends look at you like you're not living right. Because you don't do what they do no more they stuck in the same place, never want to talk about happy moments in your life but quick to throw all your wrong doings in your face. So those times I feel like my writings are not good enough, I think about where I use to be and what and who I do this for and ask do those things touch your heart? If so, then no matter what people think or say, your gift will always be good enough.

Take It For What It Is

Take it for what it is I'm speaker. I just like to speak through my poetry. I'm a person that believes people have things to say but scared too, so I'm going to make this assumption and say I think that's how God uses me. To share the untold, unwrap, and unfold the stories and situations that if I never write about it something's will never get told. I'm just talking in general no names, no personal feelings. I just tell stories I believe have happened if it's your story be bold the best step is reviving. The hurt and the pain, the frustration, and the shame. Them deep secrets and feeling you want to let out and never meet again. Just go for it, just do it, speak it to people or write it down. I have released lots of my feelings and I didn't even make a sound. I write poems, I write stories, I'm a writer can't you see. I releasing all my feelings through the gift God has given me.

Master Piece

I be in my room daily writing up a masterpiece and I'm God's Instrument that's why I call it my master piece. Thoughts in me just waiting for the moment so they can be released. My past was dark, future bright, God got a plan for my life. Just have to be patient you soon will see. And please don't pass judgment on the old person I used to be, I'm a changed man, different plan, no longer bounded by the things that use to have a hold on me. I'm free now my freedom papers was signed on Calvary, arms stretched on a cross the day my Jesus died for me. He died for my sins just a way to show his love for me. There's no way ever I could pay him back for what he did for me. But I will continue to be in my room daily writing up a masterpiece and when I do, my minds clear because my master always brings me peace.

Help Wanted

A young boy was standing on the corner with a sign I could barely read. He had holes in his clothes, no shoes, no socks, so I just assumed the sign said something that he needs. So I pulled up reached out and tried to hand him a five dollar bill. The young boy shook his head no, pushed my hand back. I was shocked, like this can't be real. I drove off puzzled, confused, I didn't understand, why did he do that? Why didn't he take the money from my hand? The next day I saw the same young boy but this time I had a twenty in my hand. The boy looked at it shook his head no and pushed back my hand once again. I quickly pulled over, hopped out my car and I walked right over. Asked the young boy why are you doing that? What's up with the cold shoulder? The young boy spoke and said, I have a place to stay, I have clothes and food to eat, I'm not here for the money, help is what I need. I'm trying to meet my

Lord and savior but no one will talk to me. They think because I'm standing on the corner money is what I need. I spoke and said, "I'm sorry I assumed, I should of took the time out to ask, but I assumed because when I see people money is all they ask." I hope I can help you now in any way I can and if I ever see a sign I can't read, I will never assume again. I just got one question for you, what did your sign really say?

He said, "Help wanted, I'm trying to meet Jesus can you help in any way."

Addicted

At age five, I was introduced to drugs. Saw something in my parent's hands that was glass like, grew up and realized it was a glass pipe. So you can say I was addicted to drugs my whole life, right?

At age seven, I was touched by my uncle. But growing up all I heard was, family is all you have in this life, I was like my family did that to me, so something just isn't right. So you can say I was addicted to sex my whole life, right?

At age nine, I became obese. My mom work three jobs, so she wasn't at the house, she just use to leave money on the counter for us to buy pizza or take out. So you can say I was addicted to food my whole life, right?

At age elevn, I got my first x-box. Played all the games with the shooting and running from the cops. Grew up and the game became reality, and I felt like I couldn't be stopped.

So you can say I was addicted to violence my whole life, right?

At age thirteen, I was introduced to Adam. Heard the story about him eating the fruit, God called it sin because it was something he forbid him to do. So you can say sin will always be in our lives, right?

Through all our sins and addictions, God died on the cross so we can have a second chance. So I guess you can say I will forever be addicted to true love for the rest of my life, right?

God, We Blame You!

We blame you, for us being born into all this constant pain, for these tears that fall like rain and for this frown that will never change.

We blame you for all these killings, sex and drug addictions. No money, no home to live in. Hungry but don't have any food up in the kitchen.

We blame you for the sick, the shut in's but that's not it, also for the ones fighting these diseases and they say "there's no cure or no way to get rid of it."

We blame you, because we have no car, can't work the job to far. Now bills added up and debt collector's searching trying to find where we are.

We blame for all these wars, all this racism but wait! I have more, for all these kidnappings, and these babies dying at a young age, we blame you for this world I call an outrage.

God: Now that's enough.

Did y'all blame me for giving my only son, the savior for when I come, who heals and restores lives, who died so that you can have a fair chance at life?

Did y'all blame or thank me for getting that job, yelling I could have done this without God. But y'all blaming me when things are wrong, when things are right y'all barely even mention God.

Did y'all blame for forgiveness, second chances at how you're living, but wait! I'm almost finished. No matter what you've been through or going through pray and repent. Mean it in your heart and that person y'all blaming "me" will be waiting with open arms to tell you, you have been forgiven.

I Blame Us!

I blame us for how we living, we preach it but do we live it? What's your definition of a Christian? Cause I'm a little bit confused.

I blame us for loving money, adultery, and possessions we put above thee, how we play with God is not funny it's like he's being used.

I blame us for not believing, in God, the one we mistreating, can't believe we would do this. To the one that gave his son.

I blame us for playing games, we pray for forgiveness but don't want to change. It's a shame that we blame God for things that we have done.

God speaks to me,

My child I understand on how your feeling, just do your job and focus on how you're living. Let God do the reveling and I know your just trying to make a change. Even when I talk they don't listen, they're blinded and their sense of hearing is missing, no matter how much you try to help, some people will never change.

Soon I will return to earth and tell people about their lives. Since birth, some will smile, and some will cry because the things I say might hurt but, there's still time to make a change. I hope people listen to these words instead of just being the same.

Use to Tell Me

They use to tell me I wasn't going to make it,

They use to say "I was nothing."

I use to ask what's your definition of making it? Because I knew my time was coming.

They use to talk about me because I couldn't read, bad handwriting, I couldn't spell, I couldn't write.

I use to go home, lock myself in my room and cry myself to sleep at night.

They use to laugh at me, make jokes when I told them God has a plan for me. I have a gift.

They said, "You can't even read or write God don't want you, your life is pointless you're worthless."

I said, "You're wrong about me I am a child of God so that makes me something not worthless. I don't have to prove anything to you. I know God has a plan for me and I will fulfill my purpose."

I just want to let you in on a little information about myself. Years ago I couldn't read or write but God changed all that in me. I have now been writing and published four books. Everybody has a weakness and it's not right to talk down on them or rub it in their face. My weakness changed over time because I prayed, I believed, I waited and had faith. So think about your actions, watch what you say and what you do, because you never know how people will react to things you say or things you do.

Hurting Inside

Has your heart ever been broken to point you felt like it would never be healed? To the point where the happiest day of your life can still never overdo the pain that you feel? From heartache to heartbreaks you wonder how are you still going through life, tore from situations brings on heavy stress that leads to migraines, thoughts of there has to be another life. Living with thoughts of ending everything because past visions over powers your visions of a great future. Nightmares of ending it with that gun with hope of no one finding out you were the shooter. Your inside is tore into pieces, wonders of how does your heart still beat. Hurt but never show it, smiles and laughter hides it, as you live each day trying to keep it discrete. Began to do things that you normally wouldn't do to try to hide the pain. But you notice that just makes you more lonely, so when your alone you cry because your to hurt to face the shame. Thought of a better life hoping to be healed, you lean on who has never failed you, God the person who has always kept it real. You might experience a lot of pain, might even doubt. But I tell you this in order to change something you have to start one day, and since you're reading this poem you have another chance to cry out to the lord, take time and pray.

Man... I Need A Drink!

Man I need a drink, Maybe if drink a shot of Hennessey or this Tequila it will clear my mind and help me think. Or if I drink this bottle of patron this worrying and stress will leave me alone, and maybe I can get some sleep. But then I blink and pinch myself cause that's not realty. Drinking just creates a temporary person that you think is you until that drunkenness fades and you look in the mirror and realize who you're really supposed to be. Drinking bottles like you gone find an escape when your finishing drowning your liver with the poison that you think is healing juice. Always trying to use the excuse that God put this on earth for us to have a good time. Correction! God placed a lot of stuff on earth for us to have a good time, not for to get drunk, act crazy, and lose our right frame of mind. Not for us to praise a substance stripping us from our right frame of mind, leaving us with nothing. Hearing about people drinking and driving killing people but we continue to do it, like other people lives mean nothing. We continue to drink to the point where we engage in violence, sometimes even leads to us abusing our kids or even abusing our spouse. Breaking up a happy home to the point you can no longer call it home now you just living in house. Made a promise to your family and friends that you will get help but when that help comes you run and you hide, scared to fight off the temptation so you go back to drinking, still trying to find healing inside. That bottle. But what you need to do is find the root of the problem, the root of situation. Let go off all those things that you have been dealing with and are now facing. Find strength to release those things you got bottled up. Pray and ask God to guide you through this journey, letting him know that the addiction you have you now want to let go, it time to give it up and tell yourself NO MORE DRINKS!

I Wish

Sometimes I wish I didn't have to wish.

I wish my life wasn't like this.

I wish I can start over.

I wish God will send my grandma back so when I cry I could lean on her shoulder.

I wish my dad would man up and be there for his sons.

But all I can do is pray for him and wish that, that time will come.

I wish my health was better and I didn't feel no more pain.

I wish I could just give back the cards that was dealt and my hand can be dealt again.

I wish my tears would dry up and they will reverse back into my head.

I wish "I love you" was something that meant something and not just something people say just to be said.

I wish...

I'm Tired

I'm tired of being tired.

I'm tired of being sick.

I'm sick of being tired.

I just want this feeling of being tired to quit.

I'm tired of being silent, it's time for me to speak up and tell my story.

I'm tired living this selfish life, money this, sex that, I'm ready to start living for God's glory.

I'm tired of being lazy, it's time to get up and make a move.

I'm tired of being this person just so I will be liked or look cool.

I'm tired of not doing things that I know I need to do.

I'm tired of missing the message that God is trying to tell me, just believe my son I have a wonderful life ahead for you.

I'm tired, I'm tired, I'm tired and if you haven't got the message yet I'm just really tired. But you know what this won't last long because God told me that this feeling is out dated. I am a changed man and that feeling is now expired.

Mind Racing

My mind racing I lost touch with my writing mind but I'm trying to straighten up and get back in it, the cheating on women, drinking all the time is not the life I want but until I change I have to lace up my shoes and keep walking in it, I would talk about money but money is a small thing I'm facing. It's not really money, but a better life for my family is what I'm chasing. Who is he? A question most might ask about me. But I be like I don't even know cause I often question myself like who am I? Blinded by things that helps me none in life but at times it just feels so right, so that's how I see fit to survive. Trying to get married to a woman that loves me dearly but I messed everything up by not trying to change my life. Am I really telling her the truth when I say "I love you" and nothing can and never will come between us two, or am I'm lying because I'm scared and I have nothing else to do. Will I ever be different so I can find the things I'm missing and focus on my life and my true loves and missions? As hard as it is I just want to say I'm sorry for being sorry and doing everything I have did. It's time to move on so I'm going to leave. I'm saying sorry with this poem and ask for you not to stop loving me and help me to stay strong. Change is coming.

Thoughts

Shackled from my hands to my feet, a war between heart and mind. Heart trying to lead the mind, but the mind is trying to find a way to shake off defeat.

Defeated by a constant struggle of wanting to make a change, but always getting pulled back into old habits.

Stuck between wanting to live life at a fast pace but see failure in the end. With understanding that slow and steady will lead to victory, similar to the story about the tortoise and the rabbit.

Constantly asking self how do I write about a life of change but change seems so far from now, questions of if there really is change if so, now the questions are, where? What? Why? And how?

I know one day my time will come when I become the man I'm supposed to be, the only thing is, tomorrow is never promised and thoughts of will I die first or will change come and the world will get to see. The man they were destine to see.

Blessed to wake up knowing that I could of died in my sleep last night. Thankful for a second chance hopefully this time I will get things right.

If I Was Rich

I wonder if I was rich would I still write poetry? Maybe if I was rich more people would support and show more love for me. I wonder if I was rich would people care more about me? Or would that just create more haters, more enemies, and would I still have people that doubt me? I wonder if I was rich would I let money take over me? Or would I have matured and understand it's just a paper substance, And refuse to let it take control of me. I wonder if I was rich but you know what I'm not rich and probably never will be, so if you're waiting for that to love and support me, forget it! Because if that's what it take then that's something I don't want to be. I want to be loved for who I am not what I have. I want to be supported by what I love to do not what it can get me, but I understand in today's society riches is the key to success. But I tell you this, I would rather be poor and loved then have riches

and be lonely and depressed. I wonder...

No Words

Sometimes when I have no words

to say or write I just close my eyes

and tell God THANK YOU!

Who's Burning You?

You see in life you get more burned by people then the stove. So when my grandma told me don't play by the stove or else you're going to get burned
I didn't listen. Played by the stove and got burned, learned a lesson but maybe that wasn't the lesson I should a learned.
Maybe I should a learned that people will play with your heart,
tear it apart, scar you so bad that even when you heal there will still be a mark.
And it haunts you, got you so scared, that you scared to love, scared to trust.
Got your mind so messed up that you don't want to live, suicidal thoughts but you tell yourself that's extreme so a lot of times you just quit and give up.
Wishing upon a star because you tell yourself maybe you

just need a little luck or maybe just a few bucks, so you can get away, then you realize that there is really no escape.

Hoping for a tragedy,

so can you can catch a case of amnesia so all the thoughts and bad dreams you will no longer have to see.

All and all you wake up thanking God for blessing you with another day to see.

Understanding that struggle leads to success so you have to deal with it, you have to face it, face reality.

Friends Or Nightmares?

I was always told to follow my dreams, but I'm like how when my life is filled with a bunch of nightmares, a bunch people saying they got your back but deep down inside they're the ones stabbing you in your back cause in reality they don't really care. A bunch of people trying to trip you to make you fall and when you do they try to kick while you're down. Made a promise that they will always be there but when you're at your low points in life, they're nowhere to be found. A bunch of clowns is what I call them. Same people that down talk you for your situations but will never try to fix their own insecurities or their own problems. But if something bad was to happen to you they get the crying and once again, they swearing, they will always be by your side. In your mind you're like Mmm hmm, yeah okay, why would I believe you now when last time all you did was lie? But let's put that aside. You were there to hand me that liquor and handed me that gun when it was time to ride. To sell those drugs with me, and yeah when all those girls wanted to party you were right there with me. Now that I think about it that's not the people I want around. I want people that's going to hold me accountable for my actions and keep me away from things that's tearing me down. Friends that pick me up when I fall and encourage me to fight harder and to stand firm on the next go around. As I pray and ask God to place those people in my life. I thank him for the friends I have now and thank him for taking those nightmares out my life.

Let It Out

I use to hold stuff in specially the things the hurt me, and things that I have been through.
So when it's come to writing it's not just a craft, I use my gift as a tool, I can use to vent through.
People ask me do I write things down. I tell them no, it's all on my mental because God put these words in me way before I could even hold a pen or pencil.
 I'm just telling you about my life tune in and be a part of it, yeah I know sometimes you only get a sneak peek or previews, you even might just get the start of it. But I'm just trying to reconnect and rekindle the relationships from family and friends I departed with.
My last name is Goss but I'm ken of many more, so in the family I'm just a part of it. Family reunions is just an event to build the fire and I attended because I play apart in it, don't want to be the whole thing I just want to be a little

spark in it. We are building a fire just to keep warm so when tempers start rising I bring out my bible and my note pad because that's a part of my survival kit. I love my life I love everything and everybody in it. Once upon a time an old head said "young boy stay focused you have a gift God blessed you." From that moment I knew I was God's Instrument and I was blessed and I didn't have to sneeze so don't pass me no Kleenex or no tissue. People ask me if I'm sick I say "no" I'm just ill with the pen, I knew a human could be, but I never knew two items my pen and my pad would ever be my best friends. Well I had fun writing this I enjoy everything I do. My advice is don't hold stuff in because you never know who needs to hear you or who's dealing with a similar situation just as you.

Share It

I been abused-share it

Molested-share it

Addicted to drugs-share it

Bad parent-share it

Homeless-share it

Jobless-share it

No car-share it

Had an abortion-share it

Been to jail-share it

I was a prostitute-share it

Addicted to sex-share it

Watched pornography-share it

Dealt with masturbation-share it

I use to steal-share it

In love with money-share it

Tried to commit suicide-share it

I been saved-shared it

Believe in God-share it

Have a lot of faith-share it

New life-share it

No matter what we have been through or dealing with God can save us from those things. Find comfort in the Lord, ask for his forgiveness. After you get help and realize you have a wonderful testimony, be proud and let someone hear about the goodness God has done for you. Can't nobody tell your story like you so why not just SHARE IT!

Good Will

We have been stepped on and abused, ridiculed and misused. Laugh at, feels like our heart was thrown in a trash bag with no recovery or any intent to be reused. People done tore us apart feels like they just gave our body parts to the good will but I will find the good will in good will because I'm a part of God's good will, so no matter what I go through I will do good. So if the world is against me and my back is against the wall I will still preach the gospel through my poetry, poke my chest out and stand tall. Might slip a little bit on this journey but trust and believe I will not fall. Because even with my mess ups, back slides and screw ups God reigns supreme and for that I will not give up. They say, "One man's trash is another man's treasure." So when life threw me to the world God found and saved me through my poetry, to me that was pretty cleaver. Couldn't read as an adolescent but now have writing four books I would say that that's a blessing.

So remember this, if you ever feel broken or unable to be used, pray to God and believe. He will answer and show you how he wants you to be used.

No Money

Money was in controlling of me... No!

Money had a strong hold of me ...No!

Money was my idol... No!

Money was the closest thing I called God so there's was no point of me going to church or even reading my bible...No!

Money was my best friend ...No!

Money was there ...No!

Through the good times and bad times money stuck with me over the years ...No!

Money was my motivation... No!

Money got me out of certain situations... No!

Money showed me that without it I can't live or deal with the things I was facing

 No Money! No Money! No Money!

Since I believed and worshiped money so much I had no

one to call or talk to. Life got so hard and I thank God he never left me. He was there when I had it and he was there when I had, NO MONEY!

Off To The Races

Off to the races, I smell victory is near, and I'm running faster than usual because they say you run faster when you run out of fear, and I'm scared. But can you hear it? The crowd cheering, their clapping me in. All my life people have been calling me a loser, so I'm celebrating after this win. Because they didn't think I could do this, they didn't think I could win, just like they didn't believe Jesus when he said "when I die I will rise in three days so don't be surprise when you see me again." And that's how it happened. Crucified, died, and then rose after three when I heard that story all I can think of was two words mission complete. That story hit something in my body, it touched me real deep, felt like even though I won the race didn't feel like my mission was complete. So instead of celebrating I went back to the drawing board I had to look deep down inside and ask myself what I was even in the race for. You see God had a mission, he had a plan, and he went forth, but now that I think about it I did all of this for self-worth. I quickly asked God to forgive me because I went about it the wrong way. I came to the realization that I don't need to be in the lime light, I just need to focus on how God will view me at the end the day. So when you're doing God's work don't worry you might not win or come in the first place, but if you ask me now I believe that God was happy with me trying my hardest and just finishing the race.

Mixed Feelings

I mixed my feelings up in this bowl they call life and I'm starting to feel like the ingredients may be a tad bit off. One cup shame, three cups of pain, started to mix that with a lot of things on my chest that I needed to get off. That still wasn't right, so I let it sit to marinate over night, hopefully when I wake up everything will taste just right. Still didn't work, so I poured in one fourth of hurt, a teaspoon of tears, and a tablespoon of fears. Added two drops of smiles, a box of turnaround, put some frowns in a measuring cup and told myself this has to be enough. But it wasn't, so I dumped it all out and I started fresh. This time I added some bad, more good, and through in some precooked of "I'm blessed". Few cups of love, a gallon of faith, and I was in my zone so I put in three fourths of hugs just because. Sprinkled in joy and a pinch of forgiveness. Put it on my plate of prayer and I been cooking up this recipe ever since. So when you're cooking up your feelings and your ingredients are all mixed up, don't just put what you think goes in the pot take time and pray. God will show you how to hook your meal up. It's Dinner time.

You Gotta Go

For years I have allowed you to be in my life. You broke my spirit, made me cry, you even made me turn on the things and people I love.

For years you manipulated me to do things even know I they were wrong. Oh go have sex, smoke and drink, you know you want to tag along.

For years you have got me further and further away from finding myself and finding my true identity. Told me you knew what was best, you told me you were a friend of me.

For years I listened because I was scared to take a stand and make a change. But those days are over and I will stand and let you know I'm tired and I will change.

For years I have been this person because I didn't want to be different, but sometimes it's ok to be and I figured out that that's what I was missing.

It's been years since I kicked Satan out my life and chose to walk with Christ. The one who died for my sins, the one never left me even though I wasn't living right.

Even though it's been years the enemy still tries to sneak in and try to get me to think about the times that we spent. But I pray and shake that off because even though I thought those things felt good there's no better feeling then the love God sent, Jesus Christ

As Far As It Goes

As far as writing books go I started with a starter kit. Went through a lot of pain in my life, gave up on it but since I started I will finish it. That means I'm not stopping at book 4 five, six, or seven I will write till I d i e, DIE and meet my lord in heaven. They say, "With joy comes pain," sometimes sunshine brings rain, but I feel like I'm living with one emotion always the same weather nothing will change. It's gloomy out here, dark, I'm searching, where's the light? Clean my glasses, turn on auto focus but still have no sight. Blinded. Wish I can fast forward my life to see to how this ends instead of going back changing things, no erasing or rewinding. This is a long journey but I have to keep moving, because give me a purpose to fulfill so I'm keep doing what I'm doing. God chose this path for me, he leads, I just keep walking straight. One foot before the other staying focus, steady pace. This time I will finish no quitting or turning back, because my God never quit plus I wasn't made like that. FINISH

Don't Quit

I hate life I don't want to be here at times I just wish I would die.

Feels like I'm alone in the world, in my times of need I have no one, no shoulder to lean on, and no one to wipe my eyes when I cry.

I find my giving up because trial and error just seems like it puts me further back.

I try and I try but still I missed up so I just quit trying, putting an end to all that.

But where does that leave me, with more bad thoughts, more false hope, all these things that mistreat me.

Breaking down to the point I don't want to get back up because in other words I'm letting my situation beat and also defeat me.

My sight of faith is gone I'm losing hope I really feel like my life is over.

Weighed down by the struggle of life, my heart cold, and on the road of being colder.

I know God can heal me but trusting and believing just seems so far away.

Never felt this low in life and I know holding on to my faith is the only way.

But what do I do when I feel I was left all alone.

With nothing or nobody, just a pad and pen was the only thing I can call my own.

The fight will continue hopefully I will continue to fight back.

Understand and believe that without God I wouldn't have made it this far, so I need to pick myself back up and know that God will forever have my back.

He's There

When is the last time you just looked up to the sky and said "Thank You!" To the Lord for everything he has done and for all the times he has blessed you. Even as a non-believer he was there for you. Through the back tracking and relapsing. Even through the greed and lust God still cared for you. Died on the cross and then rose again to show his love for you. God didn't ask for anything in return just for you to believe in him, so he can show you his unconditional love for you. He wants you to go to church, read his word, follow his commandments basically, God just wants to spend time with you. So give God the time he deserves, because God does so much for us that we don't deserve. God is calling you to him. He signs are clear just listen to his voice, cry out open and up your arms. The path is drawn out the key is in your hand all you have to do is reach out and open up the door. Walk through.

Thousand Words Intro

They say a picture is worth a thousand words, but how much is it worth if you wrote a thousand words about the picture?

Thousand Words

My journey started off rough, small guy, real shy, but deep down inside they didn't know I was tough. Not tough to the point where I wanted to fight, tough to the point that I survived through the tears and pain I dealt with every single night. Tough through the shame as I looked in the mirror and blamed myself for the reason my daddy didn't want me. Tough through the phone calls on my birthday that never came. Tough through the sunshine I couldn't see as I sat on the edge of my bed, staring out the window, vision blurred as my tears hit the window and fall down as if it was rain. Tough through the stories I had to hear as a kid. The wrongs that my father did, my mother did, questions as why would anyone want to do these things to their kids? Moms changed a lot as I got older over the years, we started talking more, opening up. Some conversations were deep, even brought on a few tears. I always wondered if I could see life through my mama's eyes, what would it look like? I closed my eyes and start to image a life of things that didn't seem so right. Moms did a lot as a single parent even though she had her own little mix ups. Grandma raised us too, showed my mom what a mother was. So moms changed some things, put her kids first and told herself that old life, it was time to give up. She worked three jobs to provide for her kids, to me that's something a true parent would have done for their kids. Marshall is the oldest so he had play the father role. Big brother but also dad, had to show us the right things to do, also the right way to go. Being the oldest he experienced a lot. Some things good, some things traumatizing, putting him in situations he didn't want to be in. Through heartache and pain he discovered his outlet, writing, a way he can release feelings and it also helped him find his identity. It's crazy how much we are alike and he's ten years older than me, my twin. Maurice was next, second oldest big bro thought me a lot. How to dress, how to make a plan to success and never give up till I made it to the top. He had a rough life, finding himself, fighting to try to fit in, moved away at eighteen to Atlanta in search of a life to be different. He loves it there with the plan to never move back. If you ever got some spare time check out my bros internet show, it's called "The boys next door" and be looking out for Moe. Marcell was the third son lived a life of many things, some things typical, even had the hoop dreams. But God changed all that and showed Marcell what his calling for him really means. Marcell began to call himself Purpose for a purpose that has never been told. Until he got closer to God and God showed him a different path for the NBA dream and Marcell's true story started to unfold. From a lifestyle of pain, anger, and a little shame, he began to rap and his life started to make a tremendous change. At a younger age he struggle to read and write but you see our plans may be different than Gods plan and blessed Marcell and now he's doing alright. He was the closest one to me. So he's my definition of a best friend and yeah I'm his little brother but our friendship is something that can never be broken, no matter how much we bend. I'm the baby boy but we have a baby sister N'tesha. At about two months she got meningitis and it forever affected my little sister. It caused her to become deaf. I was hurt when they told me she lost her hearing. She never heard me tell her I love her, man! That's a hurtful feeling. She was the people's favorite growing up, she was the only girl. Got away with everything couldn't do no wrong, I loved babysitting my little sister had no problem staying home. Graduated from Cleveland high school and went back to work there part time. Dedicated some of her time giving back teaching the students how to sign. She lived a normal life, dance team, even played basketball. Worked normal, had to prove to the world that even deaf she can do it all. She's all grown up now, she's about to be a mother. She the best sister, I wouldn't trade her in for nothing and even though she don't listen sometimes I'm happy to be her older brother. Saved grandma for last the backbone and the head of the family, she taught me to keep moving towards what I believe in even if nobody understands or believes me. She was always trying to keep peace within the family, protection, give advice, whatever she had to do for the family. Sweet potato pie is what kept us together at family functions, grandma use to make them and we would sneak and hide one for later in the oven. My grandma was an encourager, strived to be the best mother, grandmother, wife and best friend. Helped out whenever, with whatever if she could she would, she was always the one willing to lend a hand.

Family was the most important thing to my grandma. Seeing the family together is everything she would have ever wanted. So I will strive to do what I can, no matter what it is, no matter how hard it is. Because I know my grandma and that's not what she would have wanted. R.I.P Grandma Lizzie B Varner. They say a picture is worth a thousand words but how much is it worth if I wrote a thousand words about the picture.

Bonus Poems

Bully

By God's Instrument

Bully, bully leave me alone, I just want to go to school, study, have fun, and go home. It's not right that I have to get picked on because I don't have the nice things or the nicest home. Yes my clothes might be dirty or my shoes might not be new but I'm happy for the things I have just like you are happy for the things you have too. Yes I might be short but I will stand up for what's right, no more going home sad crying myself to sleep at night. Today I will take a stand for all of those who have been in a similar problem, time to brainstorm on ideas on how to solve them. This was just a little poem I wrote for a student that was having problems at school with another classmate. It's sad to see these young children experience things like this. So parents, family members, staff, and community. Take it serious if a kid says he's being bullied. I'm tired of seeing kids end their lives because they feel no one listens or cares. STOP THE BULLYING!

Acceptance

By God's Instrument

Acceptance, perception who are we really? We live in a world where the television and video games blind us; social networking has taken over so now that defines us. Every now and again we gain some sense and self-acceptance, reminds us that we don't need those things. Television creates this image that you have to look this way or have all this money, but when you look that way and get all this money you still feel empty and emptiness is the first cousin to lonely. I don't know about you but I don't like the way that sounds. And 100% guarantee I don't like how that feels. So accepting yourself for yourself is the only way you should feel. You shouldn't have to worry about what others say or how others feel about you. We all have our own unique things about us and that makes us who we are, so before you accept what the media says accept yourself just the way you are.

Controversy

By God's Instrument

Now I know some of y'all are confused and are questioning your motivation to praise God in this dying world. Questioning God like: How you going to let someone just go in that school and kill all those little boys and girls? Questioning God like: How you going to let somebody go in to that movie theater and in that mall and shoot people just to say they did something? Killing all those innocent people that had nothing to do with nothing. Now I know some of y'all are sad, mad, and I'm angry just like you, but we can't keep blaming Jesus on things that humans do. I guess when there's a tragedy or disaster in the world blaming God is the thing to do huh? But since people say there is no God, I guess there isn't any point to even blaming Mohammed or Buddha. I'm just speaking the truth. My advice is if you're a believer just keep on believing. Because God's not the one out there misleading or mistreating. And I'm not trying to be selfish, but for y'all that's blaming, when have y'all stopped to thank

God that y'all still breathing? There's a lot of killings and other tragedies going on in the world and it's angering me. So let's join our fellow believers in our communities and pray for the things that we don't see on TV. So if you're still confused or questioning your motivation to praise God in this dying world. Ask yourself this one question, how would your life be if Christ didn't die for this world?

Heart To Heart

By God's Instrument

As the sick gets sicker we sit back and watch. Let's stand up and see what we can give, see what can we do so that this would be stopped. We use prayer as a shield so we don't have to reach in our pocket books, but we buy videos games and party all the time. Not knowing a dollar a day is all it took. Shook, because the face of reality is now face to face with you, staring at you, waiting for you to make a move, waiting to see what you going to do. The selfish mind is reveal, and it shows if you really care. It shows that if it doesn't build up your church or your organization then you won't support or even be there. So sad, but claim to be believers always yelling God has the upper hand, but when face with a situation outside your comfort zone you run, you hide, because you scared to take a stand. I'm not going to sit here and say I'm always there or I always give, But I have realized that selfishness gets us nowhere, and maybe I can't give money but I can give a hug or give a smile, give something to show that I care.

Stop Lying

By God's Instrument

Stop lying to the congregation, be truthful with them. Sweeping things under the rug that's not doing nothing but hurting them. They walk around the church like nothing is wrong, choir director's gay, and the pastor knows it but don't say nothing, just up there clapping and singing as the choir director lead that song. Now don't get me wrong I love everyone and I don't have nothing against gays, all I'm saying is God don't like it, and we should try to help the situation instead of keeping things in the closet. Just so the church won't get looked at a certain way. On another note let's get back to the basic, a lot of churches are built on money and fame, let's just face it. Motives all wrong, teaching the half-truth, some pastor's do what I called "positive preaching" that's when the say" things are wrong or God don't like it". But don't show it in scripture so where is the proof. I was always told if it's not the whole truth then it's simply not true. So make sure their preaching from the bible and be careful what you are listening to. I'm not out here to try to bash nobody I'm just saying take some time, pray, and open your eyes. Take time to read things for yourself so you too will learn and realize...THE TRUTH!!!!

Broken

By God's Instrument

This goes out to that broken one that thought he was right but fell in love with the wrong one. Thinking that he was sent from up above she put her trust in him the boy she so called loved. So they got into a relationship having fun, living life. One day they even talked about becoming husband and wife. They laugh together, played together, and even ate together. And at times they didn't have anything to do, they talked and fell asleep on the phone together. You see everything was going good until that one sad day, when all the love stopped and the love started to fade away. The arguments started and the tears began to fall and she left all her friends for him so she didn't have anyone to call. Now she's all alone with nobody by her side with nothing else to do, she started to pray and ask God why? Why is this happening? What went wrong? Wasn't he sent from you? If so, why is our love not strong? Then God said, "My child I tried to speak to you and you didn't want to listen and that's why the love you thought you had is now gone and now it's missing." "My child the signs were clear but you didn't focus in and instead of you putting your trust in me you put all your trust in him." "Now you see why I wanted you to wait and I hope you learned your lesson so next time you won't make the same mistake." Then the girl spoke and said, "God I want to thank you for showing me who I am and if I ever fall in love again I will put my trust in you and never put my trust in him."

My proverbs 31

By God's Instrument

Now I would say she's one in a million, but I know you've heard that millions of times so saying that would just be cliché. So instead I will say she's worth more than rubies a virtuous woman created perfectly for me, I guess you can say God created her my way. Never thought we would ever make it, so I never thought once about us being together. You know someone that's there through the ups and the downs, the smiles and the frowns, someone that's there through the sunshine and stormy weather. Two different lifestyles but it seemed like we shared similar views and I didn't think that one day we would be writing our vows together that first day I met her in grade school. Through years of waiting, struggling, doubts and wanting to quit. We stuck together and had faith because we knew this was a gift from God, so giving up just wasn't it.

God has blessed with me with something beautiful, something rare just for me. And I wouldn't trade her for the world, no fancy car or no amount of money. My life has changed for the best, I wouldn't have wanted it any other way. And through the ups and downs, smiles and frowns, through sickness and health for rich or for poor. With the love of my life I will forever stay.

Why Me? Intro

The next sets of poems are from my upcoming play titled Why Me. This play is about two young ladies that lose their innocents. One gets through it and the other, well she has a harder time. Please prepare yourself before reading them due to the topic. It may be a sensitive subject for some.

Why Me? (Joy)

By God's Instrument

Something happen in my life that I really don't want to share, because sometimes in my life I feel alone like no one's there. Who really can I run to? When I'm having different problems, is there anybody out there? Who really can help me solve them? So I searched and I searched for many months and many years. I felt different feelings, I even experienced different fears. You see my main fear was a man because he used me in many ways. I couldn't even live my life because the thoughts affected me for many days. But still I searched and I searched to find the one special friend, the one I could tell my story of why I trusted no man. Then one day my searched finally came to an end I found that special person and to my surprise, it was a man. It was a man they call Jesus and he helped me so much. He brought me into His arms so I felt

His love and His grace through His very touch. So I gave my life to God and everything started to come out. But then God asked me that one question, He said, "Who was the man you was talking about?" I said, "That man took my innocence and I don't know why, so every time I see a man a tear forms in my eyes." I really couldn't avoid it I didn't see it coming but only if I had that one warning, my mind would have told my body to start running. I really couldn't stop him it was really no escape. I tried to scream for help but it was already too late. You see, I tried to slip away but he held me down real tight. And I tried to push him off me but he was too strong for me to put up a fight. So I'm screaming and I'm screaming, but in his eyes it was like he didn't even care. And all I could think about is, "I wish someone was there." I really couldn't believe this man was taking my innocence but I know somebody had to be there, there had to be at least one person that witness this. After it was over, he told me about one other. And I bet he didn't even know that we were birth by the same mother. Still in shock, all I can do was pray and ask God to save me on that very day.

Why Me? (Fear)

By God's Instrument

Something is happening in my life that I really can't explain like the day I lost my innocence since then my life hasn't been the same. Since that day I been lost still yet to be found and I often question myself why me? Why did my life have to get turned upside down? I never been so hurt, I never felt so much pain. I just wish I can erase the memories, the guilt, and all the shame. Why did he pick me, why couldn't I fight back, why was I all alone? Why did I leave the house that day, WHY! Why questions began to form? I started to blame myself I tell you the things that happen to me I wouldn't wish that on nobody else. Every time I think about it, it just replays in my head. I cry and scream till I fall asleep but when I wake the visions are still in my head. The hands over my mouth, the ropes that tied my legs and hands. The black eyes, the tears from my eyes,

I even picture the blood from between my legs. The consist cry for help that nobody can hear because I'm crying from inside. Are the thoughts of this going to ever end would I even see the outside? It only lasted about five minutes but five minutes turned to forever. I was released, told myself I wasn't going tell nobody ever, never, never. Yeah, that has happened just hope one day I can release it from my mind and I will be free at last.

To be continued…

Restored

By God's Grace

In the beginning it was stolen. My innocence as a child. And the unwanted grief has strived me to the nights of rubs that made my world seem as a dove. A dove in a pool of blood racing to drink the fountain of dirt. And never ending touches that keep my mouth shut. To protect the private I had known unexamined by other men. Slaved down into a bed of rocks and the legs of jello. All I wanted was for someone to say hello to this girl that hurls every time a man looks at her and not in her eyes. I feel for the girl that has be beat to perfection to please the unpleasable people. Yes I have found myself in this man. The one that everyone claims to have the master plan. I gave him a chance even though now it's hard to trust because the man that abused me was a man my family loved. For my heart was broken with no seeds to grow no flowers to water and no air to breathe. For long I have held this within without shielding truth. No one asked so I did not tell but God had other plans. To bring up my testimony to encourage and inspire others. God put peace into me but did not take pieces of my body to do it. And as I shed this truth to you God has bloomed my flowers to prove that He cares and you're not alone in this world of fear. Fear to stand up and yes I too know what you've been through. As I look back now I can say thank you. Not because I got to experience these things but because I am saved from them now and these things no longer hold me back from being free. Free through the whips that striped His back. Free through the spit that was spit on His face. Free through the nails that ran through His wrist. I am restored through the sacrifice of Christ amen.

Character, Courage and Commitment
By Rebecca Taylor

In my life my character has been altered
I'll be the first to admit it's been a hit and miss-
But as a result of living to tell my story I know my character says I will stand up for myself and I'm a speak up for my friend type of chic.

I, Rebecca Taylor, swear to tell the truth, the whole truth and nothing but the truth- so help me God today-
I'm here to talk about character, courage and commitment in a transparent kind of way.

Now courage came to me on an accident, I was tested and tried, its true-
I'm a survivor of domestic violence, I was in love with a man that beat me black and blue.
But courage came saying that's it, girl you had enough-
Made me pack my bags and what was left of my soul for a road I knew would be rough.

Adversity built my character, it brought me close to myself-no lie-
I put R. Kelly on repeat in my mind- I believe I can fly.

So this is about my commitment to myself to fight till the bitter end-
About holding strong to my courage and character even when it seems I can't win.
Commitment to winning the war although the battle is lost-
Commitment to push for excellence and doing it at all cost.

Character, courage, commitment- about my life, I'll never give-
These few lines serve as a thank you to God for giving me permission to live.

Silent Cry

By: Duoshun Pledgure

If you could walk in my shoes and see the depths of my pain

And feel the fear that races hard through my flesh and my veins

Taste the pressure when it's oh so fresh in the presence of shame

And try to make sense of it all with what's left of your brain

Hardships and challenges fester with every day break

Questioning my realities feeling like I'm a day late

And a dollar short with such solemn retort

Close to hope in my opening notes they've stolen my solace for sport

My silence is coarse but it's screaming so loudly

Still I find my freedom of speech alluding such logical thought

You've got me, I'm caught, delicate and fragile

Maybe now you'll see I'm not so eloquent and agile

I stumble and babble as one who's embattled

As if this fortress I choose mustn't be viewed as a crumbling castle

Tears welling up so much agony in this wonderland

If I could only find the words, I need grace from the Son of Man...

Young Boy

By God's Instrument

I asked the young boy was his father still in the picture, caught me off guard when he showed me a wallet size. He start shaking, you can tell his heart was racing, eyes glazed as tears formed in his eyes. Tells me this story of how his father left him, made him another statistic in a world that doesn't always accept him. Teachers and staff in the school don't understand his pain or can relate to him so they call him a problem child and start to reject him. So if it takes a village to raise a child, he must be living on an island of his own because it wasn't just his father but also his community that left him. A shame, and no disrespect to protesting things that's happening around the world but when will we take a stand in our own neighborhoods to make a change. We got young boys in our own city with their arms stretched out, crying for help, and people walk right by them scared to lend a hand to me that's kind of strange. Strange because the same young boys they scared to help, they talked about on social media and blast them on the news. Yelling this gang violence has to stop there must be something we can do. But you can't, because nowadays community centers are about money and politics, and if you don't got that five dollars to go play hoops in the gym you get kicked out of it, basically sending them right back to the streets and then people want to get back on the news and say they need to stay out of it. Man this is making me sick, we need to have things for these young boys to do, not robbing them for what most of their parents don't have this isn't making any sense. But I guess the rich gone stay rich, the poor gone stay poor, and these young boys still gone stay lost until father's step up and the community helps out that much more.

Where is the love?

Erase These Thoughts

By God's Instrument

Depression sometimes takes over my body and I seem to lose control of it.

Life moves at a faster pace with not even a chance of me grabbing a hold on it.

Trying to find myself but seem to be lost in the wrong mind.

Thoughts of bettering my life and moving forward pops up but I fall back into the same stuff leaving those thoughts behind.

Wondering who we will be there for me in my times of need or loneliness.

Wondering if I was to leave this state or even die will I truly be missed.

Hiding behind false images to gain likes and acceptance.

But telling myself, "I don't care what people think I'm me!" And I take each day as a blessing.

Will I love someone and they love the same way back?

Or will I keep setting for the same ones the ones that say they love me but sex is really where their minds are at.

Lost in a fairy tale my life feels like movie a but this can't be downloaded or bought.

If only I was a great inventor. I will build a time machine, go back in time and erase all these thoughts.

To The Top

By God's Instrument

I wrote four books I hope my family and friends noticed and they see me, because when I was younger I felt like I was gonna make it but felt nobody wanted to believe me. I couldn't read when I was younger but told myself I will still strive for this, book four title is "Mixed Feelings" cause my feelings are mixed. It wasn't hard work that paid off it was my prayers and belief, I'm just a deputy in the game had to soak in advice from God my commander and chief. Wanted to quit many times felt like nobody was supporting me, but as I look back my support came when I was slipping and everybody kept a hold of me. I'm the baby boy of my family so I was spoiled a little scratch that I know, I know I was spoiled a lot, hard headed, had anger problems, my family thought I wasn't listening but knowledge and advice is what I took and what I got. Tough times are still ahead of me but mark my words I will survive and make it to the top. Health problems tried to end my life but I'm solider and I will keep going until my heart stops. I have to make it in whatever I do I got family and friends that's depending on me, and that hard headed young boy is old, Montrell "God's Instrument" Goss the poet is who everyone was waiting to see. So watch me on this road as I take step by step, I hope you enjoyed this book but, I got something amazing coming up next.

Thanks for the support

Alter Call

By God's Instrument

Before you read this prayer, I would like you to think about your life. Think about everything you're doing wrong, and everything you're doing right. Have you ever thought about God and what he did for me and you? See Jesus went through the obstacles so that we wouldn't have to jump through hoops. The only thing you would need to do is ask God into your heart; so he can turn on your light and you won't have to keep living in the dark. Right now this is your opportunity to say this one prayer. After that you don't have to worry anymore because Jesus will always be there. Now I know you might want to wait until you go to church on Sunday, but tomorrow is never promised and you might not make it another day. I don't want you to just say this if you really don't mean it, because God knows your heart so he's going to know if you really meant it. But now that time has come where you can change your life today and when you read this I ask that you read it loud so God can really hear each word that you say.

The Prayer

By God's Instrument

God I realize I'm a sinner and I know you gave your only son to give me a second chance. God I understand that I am not perfect and I know I will never be perfect. But at this time I want to ask you to forgive me for all of my sins, for the ones I have committed and for the ones that might come about. I would also like to ask you if you can come into my heart so you can show me a new me, and so you can order my steps. God I just want to tell you thank you for everything and AMEN

Share your story

Gospelnerdzinc@gmail.com

Share your story

Gospelnerdzinc@gmail.com

Share your story

Gospelnerdzinc@gmail.com

Share your story

Gospelnerdzinc@gmail.com

Share your story

Gospelnerdzinc@gmail.com

Share your story

Gospelnerdzinc@gmail.com

Share your story

Gospelnerdzinc@gmail.com

Share your story

Gospelnerdzinc@gmail.com

Share your story

Gospelnerdzinc@gmail.com

Made in the USA
San Bernardino, CA
08 April 2018